LOVE'S BONFIRE

TOM PAULIN

Love's Bonfire

faber and faber

First published in 2012
by Faber and Faber Ltd
Bloomsbury House
74–77 Great Russell Street
London WC1B 3DA

Typeset by CB editions, London
Printed in England by T. J. International Ltd, Padstow, Cornwall

A CIP record for this book
is available from the British Library

ISBN 978–0–571–27153–5

2 4 6 8 10 9 7 5 3 1

Michael, Petronille and Thomas

Contents

Love's Bonfire

A Day with Two Anniversaries

Our aim – no mine –
was to slash the badger
(that's such bad language)
but we hit a real one
on the road to Drumquin
– too late
I saw his eyes greeny red
in the headlights
(couldn't – didn't – stop)
as the heavy *chump* confirmed
Drunquin's maybe dodgy name
but the hill the beat the walk
always inside it
– inside the drum the hill –
they promised more
– more of the same –
as – staying B&B
we sat in Harkin's Bar
looking at those two humped bookends
with the local news
going on above their heads
while they talked and drank
– one phrase I caught from that report
was *body parts*
another *cap badge*
– later we'd retire
to a lumpy bed in a room across the yard
a bed that smelt of old newspapers
– nothing was said
in that oh that dread room
a few miles from what had been your home

then like a fell arrest
I put one hand on your shoulder
but we'd no desire
no not in that damp
damp as well as dodgy bed

A Noticed Thing

The windsock by the airfield
it's hanging flaccid this evening
– hanging flaccid on its white pole
by the perimeter
I happen on it this hot humid Friday
like the way you find *a symbol*
in a poem or a novel
– something that's over- or predetermined
– something like that
or like this too obvious giant condom
with the teat snipped off
which takes us back to the static
empty windsock drained of its usual orange colour
– your name is on me it says
on me like a bullet
I can tell you're shocked
well just a tad you are
at being spoken to by a flat
– you called me flaccid –
by a flat windsock
– let me remind you
I was your image at one time
for the whole world
for everything-that-is-the-case
plus the wind rushing through it
or gulshing through it if you like
but perhaps you've moved on?
As you can see I'm all used up
like some friend you've left behind
– the world though is not conclusion
stuff that in your sock and ate it

A Spruce New Colour

It all depends on your point of view
but from mine – and I know that men
can mistake colours and shades
– from mine the new suspen-
sion bridge at Toome is puce
– puce or maybe lavender –
as it brings the new long overdue bypass
across the River Bann
like a curved – curved or semi-circular
Jacob's Ladder
which in a way is where it all began
as just sometimes I feel the wish
to drive through the village again
and see the old bridge
– or the bridge that stood in for the older one
then there's the police station
built like a barracks behind high walls and screens
the poster of the hunger striker
– young – thin beard – Kevin Lynch –
tied high on a lamp post
(I wouldn't call it a lantern)
and the black marble monument
to the young man
– a Presbyterian –
who – I don't want to say *hangs* –
who walks in the song

Elm Tree Avenue

We set up home
in a Victorian semi
in what only with hindsight
was a rather dull suburb
where we were so happy
painting walls and scrubbing floors
putting up curtains and going to auctions
at 9 every Saturday
in the grim cattlemarket.
At the back of the house
there was a small garden
the size of a diningtable
a low hedge and a gate
that led into a playingfield
where children would play
and where I once found a tortoise
our neighbours the Foxes
had lost a year back.
Beyond it was a tennis court
where one summer's evening
during the Queen's Silver Jubilee
I watched the players
suddenly drop their racquets
and stand firmly to attention
as the National Anthem
wafted from the bandstand
by the river beyond the houses.
This is another country I thought
with different manners and customs.
The English I came to see
have very good manners

– Etonians have the best –
but the Irish I've learnt
have even better manners.
Old enemies can break bread together
and shout and laugh at each other
but part the best of new friends.
This never works at an English suppertable
maybe because the English
are rather more honest
– with them what you see is what you get
– it's that plain and simple

Floragrande

Way way back – two centuries or more –
a couple of seeds made a journey
by road and by ocean from India
they were stuck in a hemp bag
hemp or hessian was it?
or maybe a carpet bag
on the Grand Trunk Road?
and those seeds changed themselves
into a great magnolia
– green waxy magnificent –
once the gardener had dibbed them
into the warm earth on the shores
the shores of Lake Como
so the years went by and those seeds
grew into something enormous
– blossoms like tulips –
a great big airy cage
somewhere between a bush and a tree
a tree or a huge bucket
plonked upside down on a beach
if you see what I mean
– c'était Pierre Magnol
qui a donné le nom
and that's the honest truth
according to Tom

Kissing Ms Khosa

Tip is touch
– as in tiptoe
or – better – on tiptoe
which is a bit like being unsteady in a church
or tin bible hall or gudwara
or it's like walking – no teetering – on stilts
or trying to talk under your breath
in a less than stealthy whisper
and being also unready
like a foal or a lamb that's just been shoved from the womb
like shit from a shovel
– a little lickspittle – yella – wobbling
on its pins in the mud wary
and doubly unsteady
as it trembles and touches the wet earth
like broken like chittering light
– yes a wee wind dog
or like that moment when the tips of our tongues first touched
which again was like walking on tiptoe
– daring but with qualms –
inside a packed or an empty church
– or tin hut I mean hall or gudwara –
wary we might trip over even though your
breasts and nipples were as yet untouched
by my fingers and palms or my lips either

so tip is beginning?
– no just the start

Love's Bonfire

One dark October evening
at the almost innocent age
of twenty-one
my love and I were walking in secret along a rough track
by the High School in Fivemiletown.
An army jeep passed down the road
(it was near the start of the Troubles).
We'd just started out
and had to be careful
not in the usual way
(that was a long way off)
but for fear of her extended family
– it was a time – it still is
of honour killings.
So we walked slowly in darkness
intent but tremulous
at this brave new so-tender thing between us
soft and tiny as a lark's egg.
We walked not quite a couple
always careful not to hold hands
(I knew that I must never
try to snatch a kiss).
So we walked slowly in the darkness
like a couple who didn't know where they were going.
By the side of the path we found
what looked like a dead bonfire.
We stared at it for a bit and then you took a stick
and began to stir
the dead embers.
From under the soft white ash
the red embers started

and as you raked and raked them
all the soft ash fell away
till they glowed and began to flame
on top of their bed of defeated ash.
So the bonfire started again and came warmly alive
as a whole big bed
of silent red embers.
I saw then I recall
that we were quite different people
– you were active
didn't want the arranged marriage
and believed we had a future
while I feared that it – the marriage
would happen for definite
and saw your mother weeping your father mad angry
the tough cousins massing
you saying no this can never be Tom
and me saying wanly
Giti I love you so dearly
and I will for always
but I see you can't bring shame
down on your family your tribe.
I had no trust we would ever
though we'd declared our love
in anguish for each other
– that we'd ever be together
for ever and ever
as the books used to say.
Forty years on
in a deep dark time
with a permanent pain always in my head
I see where that pain began.
I think if I asked you
could you call that moment back

– a moment we've never spoken of
all these long years
you'd say only
veteris vestigia flammae
– though I pray that you wouldn't.

Marked Already

I'm standing outside
– yes we've been here before –
I'm standing outside
John Melly's breezeblock bothie
on a hill above Dooey Strand
it's pinkwashed this crude hut
but dirty dinged to a boke colour
(the inside is yuk) the door
the door and the windows they're
bashed in the walls a lost yellow
on one bunk there's a pile
of smelly sheepskins with the dye
still on them like a bad mark
in a school copybook an *Aisling*
someone chucked out with the tea leaves

*

They're building a bungalow on the skyline
– here we go again –
they're building a bungalow like a barracks
way above above the bogland – scutting
    bogland that smells
always of mushrooms damp mushrooms
(here I am stepping into the same poem twice)
it's over the bogland this bungalow – over it
and the one arable acre – I say *arable*
but I mean *grazing* mean
there should be store cattle sheep
or even a donkey

on that so empty – empity – acre
– the roof? Well whether it's cut or trussed's
really no matter – the pitch of those rafters
it's too steep and the rectangle
'v breezeblocks is just too much
of a deuced a damnable rectangle
– yes a damnable rectangle

Putting the Pan On

Daithe was a headbanger
and a sort of poet
– an Ulster protestant a Unionist
so a rare kind of bird.

He lived in a soggy cottage
with Concepta in Wiltshire
(she wasn't his wife
– he'd left her years back).

We spent a night with them
drinking talking and laughing
'Here I am' said Daithe
'banging about like a bee in a tin

trying to get the pan on.'
About 10 that night
Daithe finally got the pan on
– he dropped a lump of cod

into the lardy frying pan
but didn't know that he should've
dusted it with flour
or coated it in egg and breadcrumbs.

We ate the sad pallid cod
and drank more red wine
then left in the morning
laughing all the way

through the deep green Wye Valley
at Daithe and Concepta
a happy couple
who would quarrel and make up

ten times a day.
Then last thing in our hotel
I remember you smiling as you peeled
silver foil from a bar of black chocolate

then pressing a square on my tongue
before we made love still laughing
at Daithe the bee in the tin
always about to put the pan on.

Sans Souci Park

The last big war it's
got under the skin of this house
here the scrimped and the saved
newspapers tin cans bottles
brown paper (creased) bits of string
an odd furry
hot water bottle chewed by moths
keep the house
– oh some empty cardboard boxes –
keep the house
on its always steady course
for in truth really
it's a cold water flat
among several flats on two levels
where old people live stealthily
quite naturally in the same stucco house
a house I want to call Ballykinlar
(place of the candlestick)
after the camp and the barracks
under the Mourne Mountains
hardly palatial that name
I mean Ballykinlar
and your flat it's chilled
by utility furniture
and the saved electric
– furniture that says that's that –
end of story finis
as we eat our meal
under the kitchen clotheshorse
(its cloth and woolly blade
hangs from the ceiling above our heads)

which – cloth cap maybe –
which brings back that private
squaddie from the Gorbals –
you tried to save from the gallows
– a poor shopkeeper he'd raided
– raided and pushed –
banged his head and died
then a few weeks later
winter of 43 –
Mr Justice Pierrepoint tied the noose
we need neither of us think
of that nameless kid
trying to eat his last breakfast
as – I won't to be polite
call this prog or a feed – as
we start on our meal
a single lamb shank with a few
scraps of onion or carrot
– baked in a low heat
along with some biscuit and parkin
to a recipe that's about as
basic as a ration card
– ration card or a boat deck – boat
with some cargo
braving the tide bar
like that ship in a bottle
or your too tired face
there at the window

POEMS AFTER WALID KHAZENDAR

A Caution

The night's last shifty least dregs
a fag end just before the light begins
to walk – it's the same bench – go sit
as if you don't know it
and drop that lop-sided smile –
I can see it's a fake –
try make it mean something

as you stare the dead obvious in the face
shall I reach a mug of water
into your hands?
out of the desert I want to take
no message nor doctrine – only an antelope
a shy a very gentle thing
but you'll say 'no there's no hope'
and pass the empty the heavy metal mug
back into my hands

the grievance is firm a principle
– like your silence such a chill thing
like your body – your untouched body – that's too still
but if you stammered even acted the fool
that'd be the best body armour
– it's always plain what you're thinking
especially when you try and hide it
– I say to you please please stammer
don't make this distance between us
– d'you want the silence to burst back
like some ten ton space shuttle?
– d'you want the boxthorn to have no flowers
– no waxy yellow flowers only thorns?

Being in Time

Here – you bee – wee thing
pass on by now
all the lights are fused in this –
well block – it's hardly a house
but maybe you'll make our eyes
touch the horizon again
– should that happen
the sound our feet make
'll catch up with the steps themselves
– a dithery echo that mocks
then straightens their clamping sound

let's take a walk
at the crack of dawn
then we'll maybe step a shade taller
our doors and all the frames that held them
– thresholds and lintels – we lost them all
our keys were like plasticine
and our shadows melted in the sunset
– either we stumble
or follow the wrong road on the map
(but every road there is wrong)
like Nisus
or was it Euryalus?
we none of us know
how to keep radio silence
but we know that the honey bee
is gall and nectar
– the taste of you and me

Belongings

Who entered my room when I was out
and moved the vase on the mantelpiece just a tad?
who skewed that print – a Crusader – on the far wall?
and those pages loose on my desk
they're a shade dishevelled aren't they?

of course someone's read them
and my pillow's never been dented this way
– not by any lovely head
that stray shirt I'd never leave on the floor
– some shit's dropped it

so who came into my room? who?
and who'll put the vase back exactly
as it was? who'll
straighten the mailed knight in his corner?
and who'll restore to my shirt and pillow
their full rights as citizens
of my single room?

Birds

Birds in the trees
– summer's long gone –
it's the fall still
so tight so cold
but what could be free
are those finewebbed birds
resting in your fingertips
– you make them into a steeple
then they're on the move
then marking time
in the one position
– if only they could fly way
way up and be done with it
– ock it's too cold
we mustn't we mustn't

Flashgun

There was no knowing
where the door led
nor why the plants by it
were yellow and bent
but what puzzled him most
was the roses
– they were in his face
ock intimate
and their colours gripped him like a glove

ashy and tired – get the picture? –
they look black the horses
just where they touch the cloudstuff

the point of him being here's
no way clear – he's got
a few ghosts and a coffee pot
the fur on his tongue it
makes him bare his teeth
the horizon's a needle
so's the thornbush
no it's a whole great box of them
such a prickly root

then all in a rush
he caught up with his own face
this climate plays tricks
makes it look like the trees
in the walled orchard
are occupied only by fruit
– the night's out in a flash
the night's a gonner

Force

He lords over leftovers – brock –
just in drawing it
his hand salutes the curtain
– the birds have flown off
the bushes have been bashed about
no limes no oranges
and the leaves they neither shine
nor glint

dayclean but spent
it can't complete the night
nor pull a whole day from its sock
he'd wanted it strong like black tea
so he could ask himself
shall I start out yet again?

he wanted to rub his tongue on tree bark
and ask how it happened
this chaos this mess?
was it the force of the ground
or the air?

what colours my speech he decided
is a climbing no a clinging weed like
but not jasmine

his tea's cold in its chipped enamel mug
– a labrador's nose
but his bare feet on the rug
know for sure he's a topdog

House on the Shore

We sailed the boat
almost as far
as our front door
– windwhap ropethrum
the slick ease of the tide
it was hardly a strand
– two metres just –
we walked across
into our livingroom
like we'd sailed inside
– we drank wine there
that's where we dwelt
we'd good times
oh the best of times
but it's an empty box our house
just a crate
that's been cleared out

Humping the Word Hoard

You drag your shadow behind you
like it's a ladder
or a sack stuffed with half-bricks – with halfurs –
your plain speech is like bread
– bread spliced with chocolate
(of course I'm getting this wrong
what pricks you is the wait
for that old joke Aufklärung)

the pots in your yard are too tight
– their hard glaze it won't crack –
too tight for the roots 'v your jasmine and roses
– sure they tried run up the bricks
but it's water they need
it's water they're waiting for
you can't water them with your patience

The Thin Hem

Maybe she's intending to pray
– no I can't – can't pray – it's such a drag
the sight of a woman praying
a woman rubbing the thin hem on her scarf
like a scab
it always reminds me prayer
of a woman stationed at the sink
a woman with rubber gloves
washing the dishes
– she's put bread for the doves
but they don't land at her door
while the leaves on the vine
they turn ochre – scorched –
this time of year she hurries them on
but always heavily – with unhope – it's her
loved one who isn't here
and that *isn't* is the weight
in this room
its airless block of nothing
– if he arrives
he'll split the air
like the flame on a welder's torch
but he doesn't he can't
– now all I want
is to find a fire and pour oil
right back on its flames

Letter of the Law

It's not the morning all night long
that we wanted or expected
but its evening is sure and certain
– it's a fact – it's known

do we say for a joke the ears of corn
leapt like deer on a mountain?
that each looked like a ploughshare on a mountain?
that there was even a glow on the horizon?
did we walk on soft paths – more like saltpans –
that led to one invented season after another?
– the ways they find to turn *no*
right back on its head
and still mean *n n n*
right to the end of time
– that is the time
states and peoples live in
their tines their tines ses épines
where they stick and harden

oh again and again
we know it's darkness at noon
and learn to walk without shadows

– to become our own shades – manes
aye the morning's been let soften
but it's strong enough to warn
it'll find out ways
of getting even more even

A Single Weather

They've got gaps in them the best walls
– it was a geg the way we'd grip hands
then slip through that tall – tall
and tight – gap in the wall
yes we squinched through that fissure
came back again and again we did
under fruit that was fit to burst

I could hear you trapped in your own voice
as we made sleaked talk – worse and worse –
by a well that since we were kids
no one'd drawn a bucket from ever
– unlike the sky you were never the same
and come nightfall you were different again
you felt no right to go back – both it
and the will to return
you'd let them slip

Starting from Scratch

Compared to the next generations
the first houses came to look like hovels
– some were knocked down some
turned into garden sheds but always
they carried the memory of migration
– of being at one time – time not far back –
just trailer trash and good for nothing else

the people who lived in those hovels had just
invented the cartwheel and then come
to the conclusion that their hunting and gathering
was tiring them out
– it was time for the first founding act the building
of granaries between rivers and roads
the paving of streets then the building of houses
after lines had been drawn in the dust cords
stretched between pegs and plumblines dropped
as pious shopping lists invoices bills of lading
were scratched on clay tablets and writing began
as a fixed a wholly practical thing
not soft sift or sticks in the sand
– new granaries rose like clay ovens bulbous
and motherly – it was all clay the way spades and shovels
banged out a tune that never stopped
except when night fell on the land
between two rivers – the island
al-Jazireh
that – now we know it – is Mesopotamia
its borders redrawn one countryhouse weekend
in a not quite island called England

The Pinched Stream

The stream clems to a trickle
that looks like a back alley
though it makes not a sound
which is just where you are
– right between no sound and no sound
and finding some needy person to pity
– you get into bed with her
but now you won't ever
look up at the sky when it's cloudy and dull
and predict good weather

these days you don't kid yourself
in these tight dodgy alleys
where one time a house stood
domestic like a pot on a shelf
– with neither twilight nor dawn scrake
the night's doubly
dark – it's up to no good
now you hear a noise
or you kid yourself it's a noise
you see a boat on a blue lake
and a hand like a bird waving *goodbye-ee*!
you hear rain that isn't there
hitting windows that aren't there
and before you even make a move
you can hear the noise your footsteps'll make
– it's as though fruit can choose
not to settle on the earth

The Wait

If you sit here
you'll see his face quite clearly
a spring in his step but his face
dead pale like a thorn
– a long one from a boxthorn
he'll sit at the table yes
but he'll keep in shadow
and appear smaller than he was before
– coffee a glass of water
they'll sit there and wait
– wait for ages
the coffee'll go cold
and the water'll get warm
don't think he's a stone
bare and unflèched
a figure with no face
– one that doesn't quiver
it's just that the light's gone
and dropped him in a deep pit
– maybe an hour later
he takes a sip and winces
– tepid water
he slits a smile like a paperknife
you'll see such a smile
only once in your life

now they'll crowd the light
and poke about in his darkness
– to them it's a puzzle
though they can tell that in spirit
he's gone out the door

The Sail, Again

Only to sleep for a little while
and then wake up – this
would make the pack slip from my shoulders
take that pushiness from my chest
and burst the buttons – the too-tight
buttons – tin medals – that're stuck there

was it all for nothing the thing
we launched that fell back on us?
– then finish over and done with
but now's the time to start over again

as he fell asleep his hands dithered
the blue china caught the rough
red sunset and the crack in the wall
was a real a deepening split
that headed up to the ceiling and made
it seem to come down – as per usual
the dust was a distraction

I looked on it as on all that had passed
stretched out on chairs and benches
spreading over plants that weren't there
– it was so solid the air
the frames on the walls they pulled back the de-
parted
and then the window the dark
window with no curtain showed a sail
– sure it was torn to bits
but still it led the wind

Stateless Twice Again

for Yousef Qasmayeh

They won't – they will not – permit me
– I'm a shadow's shadow –
they won't let me
be a refugee
of course I want you to know this –
or as you might say
I want that you know this
– said in your local
more than slightly menacing way
– I want you to know how
I got here from a camp
in the Bekaa Valley
where I taught myself English
– pure perfect English –
by listening to the World Service
so I could talk in your language
– it's a world service
– another nature
but here in England they won't allow me
to find or to take a job
which means I walk the streets of these cities
– London – Oxford – Manchester –
like someone who's lost the station
he's searching on the radio
all the wow the chaff the clatter
that's shrill and pitched
like a hard pea
– I mean a pea in a whistle

And Be No More Seen

The oilcloth on the kitchen table
an olive green thing – retro surface
japped with little bits of water
or if you like with bits 'v watter
and so *throughother – itchy uncomfortable*
is what you call this kind of mess
the ever so slight chaos of matter
where what you want is tightness order
– though having just said this
it's like I've wiped the oilcloth clean

Daisies/Du Barry's

The way flowers look in this North Oxford florists
– sort of Stanley Spencer that cold intense
English light on flowers and faces
white skin big waxy tulips alabaster bowls and vases
– this being here and then not quite
as my mind – Saturday morning mind – shifts
to that bar by the docks – Godawful dump
– damp rackety packed with seamen dockers rentboys hoors
where a Palm Court professor of the bottle
– Stanley Spencer's brother washed up
piano in one corner of the draughty floor
– see my mind's begun to jump
back over a little ramp or hump
that's like a stray
bit of dust on a doubly old record
– it makes ever such a tiny bump

Donegal Naif

Some hairs off a donkey
– or some hairs off of a donkey
– its tail not its hide
they're bound with white cotton
thread to a hazel twig
– if you think the paint his brush applies
to tacked canvas on this island
looks slightly wonky
then your taste's rotten
it's completely awry
as he turns the fisherman who digs
for lugworm on the Black Strand
man with a collie dog
on the sulphurous sand
at low tide
turns him into one of those local gods
who won't never die

During the Countdown

On the second day of the second month 2003
we were walking through Beeston
– it looked that Sunday
more like a wet northern
than a wet midland town
with big strange pollarded trees
on both sides of its not wide not grand
Imperial Road
– every single limbless hacked cutback trunk
was taller than the Victorian houses
and each a kind of écorché
displaced almost tarry with a blind scorched
halfconscious look
– these overgrown but somehow ambushed trees
they'd got too grand for a mere road
– maybe when their trunks were just saplings
it looked like an avenue in the making?
Now these rooted
not quite cadavers were nearly speaking back
like a tamarack a hackmatack
– that is the American the charred larch

Saggy

Rembrandt's drawing of an elephant
is yes a drawing of that mild
displaced creature a real elephant
so loose and baggy you'd never think
it belonged ever to the wild
but if you blink
you'll see it's an almost child-
like portrait of the artist
his pouchy tragic vigilant
and softened face waiting for the fist

Same Ould Strop

Benburb Eglish Caledon
– add Drumbo
(accent on the *o*)
but mind you've no rights
– no rights of knowledge
no rights of property
on that clanky sound *dinnseanchas*
they're hard nuts these placenames
– why try crack them again?
or they're bolts you can't force

Eglish but
it's softer greener
and more familiar
it's a milkygreen
nut on a hazel
or a wisp that hasn't dropped the *n*
(it was always *n* less)
– it could be a girl's name
– she has no bubs
and it's hard to place
the exact shade of her cotton dress

No Packdrill

Something to do with shaving tackle
– the brush the razor
the stick of soap
halfwrapped in tinfoil
and then the fact he was the stranger
in my house
– I should call him Roger
though he wasn't that
a canny dope
an early jogger
reminding me that objects
which are both ugly and utile
often leave you feeling slightly soiled
I saw his razor
– a bit brassy bit genital
and imagined soldiers
– raw squaddies – no style
not genteel
or I should say not gentle
but beefier a lot stronger
than I was or am
and each as obvious
as a tin of oil
– I reach out now what
six seventeen years later?
reach out to collect
my own tackle
from the glass shelf
in a hotel bathroom
and see a version of myself
touched by fear and guilt
like a face at a window

Shades Off, No Sheds

The dingy green the bulky
corrugated iron sheds and barns
they're crowding up to this
pebbledashed farmhouse on a drumlin
above the road (I'm driving to Derry)
so like the warehouses the sheds and barns they –
huggermugger way ugly –
they overlook both the road and the house
– call them warehouses or tinpot titans
dressed in dirty uniform paint
– paint applied after the raw tin
has cured its sheen over four years
in all weathers
– they're bodged these buildings
they're out of scale
and also out of place
and though I like the paint's oiliness
– almost oiliness I should say
for it's dried – matt – it isn't liquid
and it's long ceased to be sticky
– 'sdulled a bit flaky
which may be why the name *Crumlin*
comes and goes in my mind
like a bald man wearing shades
– tattoos show on his hands
when he takes his gloves off
– but those walls those doors and roofs
enclose dead space
and have none of the feel the barm
that belongs to a dwellingplace
– they're hangar pure nissen

and the house on the rise the house itself
they hold it in question
like a gang who themselves
ought to be under suspicion
– OK it's a standoff
they're windowless unlike the house
that looks as though it's studded
with little white eggs
– with sugared I want to say almonds
but that's a world
– world and a bit away
and the house stands on a proverbial
a local egg – on its drumlin
so I imagine turning the earth
and finding bits of broken delph
and those shards marking
what somewhere is called *the real presence*
– break a cup a bowl a plate
a beer whiskey or lemonade bottle
then chuck their fragments – brish –
chuck those bits of hard brittle eggshell
straight in the midden
like casualties after some battle
– can we say then that such an action begins
whatever it is those sheds those barns
are trying so hard to block out?

Something Said

It was some phrase like *level playing field*
that gunked me as he said it
I was back on the outskirts of Grimsby
– Grimsby or Great Yarmouth – but
that's not right – I was in the shit – just normal shit –
in Gedling you know that struggling throughother pit
village where we lived for half the 80s?
– its railway lines allotments dry sooty
slagheaps abattoir and that big battery
chicken farm a fox one Sunday morning
got right inside – it put 5000 heads
in its jaws and broke their necks
programmed like a soldier to heap the dead up
and yes I'd forgotten the house at the level crossing
where the oldest Falkland Islander came to stay
(he was a late Victorian aged 90)
– all this and more I got from something said
by a young man in a pale blue suit
and matching slightly shiny necktie – his
let's try to unpack this gave me the cue
to leave the room no disattend the meeting

St Hardware

A silver birch
with shivery tattery bark
that's like skin or thin paper
flickering in the wind
– chill February wind
for a moment the sky goes dark
and we feel we're in church
before the service has started
or we feel like we've sinned
as we walk past a delicatessen
in the soft the north part of town
where we let the tree
the flittery scurfy tree
teach us a lesson
– now I try offer a prayer
to St Decommission
who is also St Hardware
– a spirit whom no one
has yet set their eyes on

The Choice

Now that at last I've crossed over and left
the daylight gods on their owny own
like statues in a civic square
their stiff lips mouthing a tribal chant
all about breaking from the bonds of kin
and from that desert prison they built again
on a green hill bog desert mountain faraway
– statues dry and white as calcium or bone
for they cast no shadows and the grass
beneath them isn't quite the real right thing
under a slab of air impure air

– now that I've crossed I can see that this
is the Atlantic world ripe to the core
and like a massy cruise ship floating nine
storeys high near some rutputty Roman port
where a barearsed boy is eating a filched apple
and clocking what he guesses must be a skyscraper
– I see it now I've joined the sifting shadows on this shore
and discovered not the side itself
but the other in that phrase *the other side*
spoken in my one tight language
– here it's dark downward without form
as I drop through it spineless a hugger of shadows
like a criminal or an agent – look at me soaked
in some foreign port some dockside dive
where I could if I wanted add spit to the sawdust
and feel maybe a shade better

Shy Willows

The swallows diving and crying
above the streets and squares
picking and unpicking their threads
– sewing nothing with nothing
then the sallows the sallies the gardens
– river gardens –
I want their greens and their ochres
against those blue and white buildings
and I want the term *shaggy*
– not so far from *savage* –
soaked into its silks